W9-BNL-190

Valparaiso Public Library
103 Jefferson Street
Valparaiso, IN 46383

PORTER COUNTY LIBRARY

Lewis and Clark

Valparaiso Public Library
103 Jefferson Street
Valparaiso, IN 46383

By Lisa Wade McCormick

Subject Consultant
James D. Harlan
Program Manager and Senior Research Specialist
Geographic Resources Center
University of Missouri
Columbia, Missouri

Reading Consultant
Cecilia Minden-Cupp, PhD
Former Director of the Language and Literacy Program
Harvard Graduate School of Education
Cambridge, Massachusetts

Children's Press®

MAY 3 1 2006

JJ   920 MCC   VAL
McCormick, Lisa Wade, 1961-
Lewis and Clark /
33410008844799

Designer: Herman Adler Design
Photo Researcher: Caroline Anderson
The photo on the cover shows Lewis and Clark.

Library of Congress Cataloging-in-Publication Data

McCormick, Lisa Wade, 1961–
 Lewis and Clark / by Lisa Wade McCormick.
    p. cm. — (Rookie Biographies)
    Includes index.
  ISBN 0-516-25039-6 (lib. bdg.)   0-516-21443-8 (pbk.)
  1. Lewis, Meriwether, 1774–1809—Juvenile literature. 2. Clark, William,
1770–1838—Juvenile literature. 3. Lewis and Clark Expedition (1804–1806)—
Juvenile literature. 4. Explorers—West (U.S.)—Biography—Juvenile literature.
5. West (U.S.)—Discovery and exploration—Juvenile literature. 6. West (U.S.)—
Description and travel—Juvenile literature. I. Title. II. Rookie biography.
  F592.7.M33 2006
  917.804'2—dc22   2005021745

© 2006 by Scholastic Inc.
All rights reserved. Published simultaneously in Canada.
Printed in Mexico.

CHILDREN'S PRESS, and ROOKIE BIOGRAPHIES®, and associated
logos are trademarks and/or registered trademarks of Scholastic Library
Publishing. SCHOLASTIC and associated logos are trademarks and/or
registered trademarks of Scholastic Inc.
1 2 3 4 5 6 7 8 9 10 R 15 14 13 12 11 10 09 08 07 06

Would you explore unknown lands for your country? Would you fight bears and go days without food? Explorers Meriwether Lewis and William Clark did.

Lewis and Clark's adventure took them as far northwest as present-day Oregon (above).

Meriwether Lewis

Lewis and Clark led the first official group to explore the West for the U.S. government.

They made their famous journey more than 200 years ago.

William Clark

Before 1803, France owned much of western North America.

In 1803, France sold that land to the United States for $15 million. This sale became known as the Louisiana Purchase. It doubled the size of the United States.

A map showing the United States after the Louisiana Purchase

Thomas Jefferson

President Thomas Jefferson asked Lewis to explore the new land. Jefferson wanted Lewis to find a water route to the Pacific Ocean.

Lewis asked Clark to join him. They had known each other in the U.S. Army.

Lewis spent $2,324 on supplies. He bought guns, clothes, food, medicine, and even crayons.

Lewis also bought beads, mirrors, and scissors to trade with American Indians.

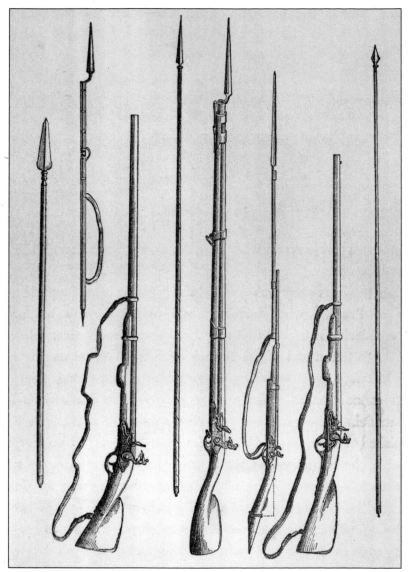

Guns and other weapons from the early 1800s

The Corps of Discovery leaving Missouri

On May 14, 1804, Lewis and Clark started their journey. They left their camp near Saint Louis, Missouri, and headed northwest on the Missouri River.

Forty-five men joined Lewis and Clark. This group was known as the Corps of Discovery. The Corps also took Lewis's dog, Seaman.

The Corps traveled up the Missouri River in a keelboat. A keelboat is a shallow boat. Keelboats were often used to float goods along a river.

Lewis and Clark built a camp for the winter among American Indians known as the Mandan and Hidatsa people. The Corps called the camp Fort Mandan. The area where Lewis and Clark stayed is in present-day North Dakota.

The Corps traveling up the Missouri River in keelboats

Sacagawea (right) with Lewis and Clark during their journey

At Fort Mandan, Lewis and Clark met a Shoshone Indian named Sacagawea (sah-kuh-juh-WEE-uh).

Sacagawea would later leave Fort Mandan with Lewis and Clark. Sacagawea became famous for her work as a translator. During Lewis and Clark's journey, she helped the Corps communicate with different American Indian tribes.

In spring 1805, Lewis and Clark left Fort Mandan and began their trip again. They traveled past the Great Falls in present-day Montana. They also crossed the Rocky Mountains.

The journey was not easy. There were times when the Corps almost ran out of food. At one point, a huge bear attacked Lewis. Luckily, he survived.

The Great Falls overlooking the Missouri River

The Pacific Ocean off of present-day Oregon

As the journey continued, the Corps traveled on the Snake and Columbia rivers. Finally, they reached the Pacific Ocean in mid-November 1805. Lewis and Clark made it all the way to the area that later became the state of Oregon.

Lewis and Clark returned to Saint Louis, Missouri, on September 23, 1806. They had been gone two years, four months, and ten days. The Corps had traveled nearly 8,000 miles (13,000 kilometers).

Along the way, Lewis and Clark discovered 300 new plants and animals. The Corps met fifty different American Indian groups unknown to people in the East.

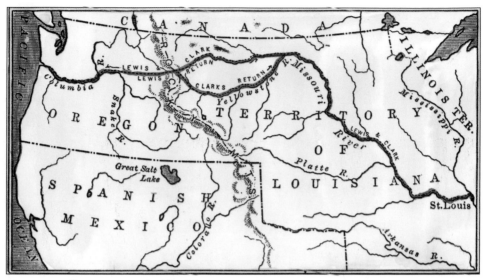

A map of Lewis and Clark's journey

Only one member of the Corps died during the difficult journey.

Lewis became governor of the Louisiana Territory (above) in 1807.

After the journey, Lewis became governor of the Louisiana Territory. He died on October 10, 1809.

Clark became head of the Bureau of Indian Affairs. This is a government agency that works with American Indian groups to discuss topics such as land, health, and education.

Later, Clark was made the first governor of the Missouri Territory. He died on September 1, 1838.

William Clark as governor of the Missouri Territory

A statue of Lewis, Clark, and Sacagawea

People will always see Lewis and Clark as heroes. Their journey helped open the American West for future explorers and settlers.

Words You Know

Louisiana Purchase

Meriwether Lewis

Pacific Ocean

Sacagawea

Thomas Jefferson

William Clark

Index

About the Author

Lisa Wade McCormick is a children's author and award-winning journalist. She lives in Kansas City, Missouri, with her husband, Dave, their two children, Wade and Madison, and their dog, Murphy. Like Lewis and Clark, Lisa and her family also like exploring new places.

Photo Credits

Photographs © 2006: Bridgeman Art Library International Ltd., London/New York: 24 (Ambroise-Louis Garneray/Bibliotheque Nationale, Paris, France, Archives Charmet French), 5, 31 bottom (National Historical Park, Independence, Missouri, MO, USA); Corbis Images: 11 (Bettmann), 8, 31 top right (Rembrandt Peale/Bettmann), cover (Alfred Russell/Bettmann), 20, 30 bottom right (Craig Tuttle); Gary R. Lucy Gallery, Inc., Washington, MO/www.garylucy.com: 15 (Lewis and Clark: Red and White Pirogues Traversing the Missouri River,1804, by Gary R. Lucy), 12 (Lewis and Clark: The Departure from St. Charles, May 21, 1804, by Gary R. Lucy); Getty Images/MPI/Hulton Archive: 27; Nativestock.com/Marilyn "Angel" Wynn: 16, 31 top left; North Wind Picture Archives: 28 (Nancy Carter), 7, 19, 23, 30 top; PictureHistory.com/Charles Willson Peale: 4, 30 bottom left; Superstock, Inc./age fotostock: 3.